HOW TO WIN WHEN SH*T HAPPENS

30 Affirmations to Build Mental Immunity in the Midst of Chaos

CHRISTAL D. JORDAN

edited by Zara London-Southern

Everything I do is in honor of the supernatural love my mother Jacqueline D. Jordan gave me as a girl child, a young lady and later as a woman of means. AJ you are always my first love. To Chanelle Edryce & Stone Erickson for being God's most beautiful and perfect gifts, and unequivocally my WHY.

To the strong women I am inspired by on a daily basis, we must continue to be iron sharpening iron. I'm honored to be your sister, friend and colleague.

Thank you to Mark Battle for believing in the power of I AM!

And last but not least to my Ace that I hope will stick around to infinity and beyond.

Foreword

In this work Christal Jordan has penned a transparently captivating tome that will touch your soul and regenerate your spirit to embrace each new day with energy, confidence, and most importantly, a renewed sense of worthiness. The release of this work, based on affirmations that Ms. Jordan has created and used to guide her own journey to a rich and rewarding life experience, could not be timelier.

HOW TO WIN WHEN SH*T HAPPENS is brilliantly organized in a flow that over the course of 30 days moves the reader from the core of self through layer after layer of fear, uncertainty, and doubt, to emerge as a stronger, more self-assured individual. The only problem you will have is controlling the desire to read the entire book in one sitting! I recommend that you resist that temptation however...

Instead, savor each day's beautifully prepared 5-course meal for a full 24 hours of reflection and meditation. I promise, doing so will change your life...

Mark I. Johnson

Life Transformation Through Goal Achievement Coach

Introduction

Have you ever wondered why some people remain full of life and optimism during tragedy while others struggle through depression, anxiety and fear? The dividing factor between these two kinds of people isn't genetic and it certainly doesn't have anything to do with luck or circumstance. We know that regardless of socioeconomic status or background race or culture, everyone suffers loss and deals with grief and disappointment. The difference is some people use the obstacles thrown their way to become stronger, while others allow those obstacles to overwhelm them until they lose their sense of self, their livelihood and even their health.

The great news is YOU have the power to decide which type of person you are going to be moving forward. The good news is the deciding factor in your becoming this new person has nothing to do with how much money you make or where your family is from. Your race, age or ethnic background have nothing to do with it. There are no classes you can take to change your outcome, no certification, and no degree.

The secret that everyone who becomes stronger through adversity knows is that their capability comes from time spent building the one muscle that carries our future. While physical strength is important and boosts confidence, it can't help you navigate the intangible pitfalls that cripple us emotionally.

The only thing that can prepare you for financial loss, heartbreak, death, illness etc. is your mental health— aka having a strong and healthy MIND. I know, I know: you are wondering what your mind has to do with coping with the issues mentioned above.

Your mind determines how you interpret everything from happiness to sadness, joy to grief to devastation.

The google definition of the mind is: the set of cognitive faculties including consciousness, imagination, perception, thinking, judgement, language and memory, which is housed in the **brain.**

According to this definition, or mind determines our imagination, our perception, our thinking, and our judgement, which all play a vital role in the way we respond to tragedy.

You should know the majority of our setbacks in life are due to negative internal thinking. If you hear bad news from someone early in the day and you digest and repeat that bad news over and over to yourself throughout the day and the evening, you will have not only convinced yourself the initial story was true but you will have diagnosed yourself with the negativity. This illustrates the power of words on our lives and most importantly our destiny.

This book was created to help you build your mental muscles, thus enabling you to internalize, digest and react to both positive and negative stimuli differently.

I believe YOU can become the type of person that overcomes tragedy without being controlled by fear, anxiety or stress. Over the next thirty days, we will do daily mental exercises also known as affirmations designed to re-train the way you process information, regardless of its stimulus.

Every day you will repeat a different affirmation 10 x while inhaling and exhaling during a self-imposed meditation time. Give yourself at least thirty minutes to read the affirmation and explanation in its entirety and then sit quietly with your eyes closed envisioning becoming the manifestation of the words. Sounds cheesy? Maybe. But I guarantee, after thirty days of building your mental fortitude you will approach everything in your life differently.

In addition to saying your affirmations in the morning, I suggest recording the words down in your phone, or if you still prefer pen and paper, on a notepad. It's important to repeat your daily affirmation whenever you encounter something during the day that triggers your stress, anxiety or any other negative emotion. As you get more days under your belt, it will become a reflex to stop and redirect your thoughts to your affirmations and move forward. Soon you will not need the affirmations: your brain will be strong enough to do this on its own.

You made the first step towards becoming a different person by purchasing this e-book! I'm excited for you to take this journey and ask that after you master it, you pay it forward by sharing it with at least one other person.

There is a famous, anonymous quote that goes, "Minds are like flowers. They only open when the time is right." I believe your purchase of this e-book suggests the time is right for you. The journey to the new YOU starts NOW! Let's begin!

1

Day 1

Affirmation:

I AM LOVE. I AM LIGHT. I AM POWERFUL BEYOND MY WILDEST DREAMS AND IMAGINATIONS.

(Close your eyes and take a moment to center yourself. State your affirmation boldly and then inhale deeply and exhale. Repeat 10x)

I AM: Two of the most powerful words, for what you put after them shapes your reality.

— Gary Hensel

WELCOME to the first day of the journey to the new YOU.

What better way to start than realizing that YOU possess the power! Your mind is much like your physical body in that while it may be genetically blessed to some extent, true strength, the kind that is competition-worthy, comes from consistent training and discipline. You would not expect to win a marathon without training your body, so you should not expect to be successful over the course of your life without training your mind.

TOGETHER WE ARE REPROGRAMMING your mind so that it's equipped to manifest the reality that you choose for yourself. In order for your mind to be strong enough to change your perception we must start at the basics. Defining this new version of yourself will not be easy. You will need to stop yourself throughout the day and repeat today's affirmation.

WHENEVER YOU ENCOUNTER an obstacle or become aware of self-doubt, stop yourself immediately and repeat today's affirmation. For you to be able to overcome the insurmountable odds, you must believe that YOU are more powerful than any obstacle that crosses your path.

Congratulations on a powerful Day One!

2

Day 2

Affirmation:

I AM WORTHY OF ALL MY DREAMS AND DESIRES

(Close your eyes and take a moment to center yourself. State your affirmation boldly and then inhale deeply and exhale. Repeat 10x)

OUR DEEPEST FEAR *is not that we are inadequate. Our deepest fear is that we are powerful beyond measure. It is our light, not our darkness that most frightens us. We ask ourselves, 'Who am I to be brilliant, gorgeous, talented, fabulous?' Actually, who are you not to be? … We are all meant to shine, as children do. We were born to make manifest the glory of God that is within us. It's not just in some of us; it's in everyone.*

— *Marianne Williamson*

THE IDEA that we are worthy seems like a simple one but it's one of the biggest hindrances on our journey to success. Often we equate our value to our family background or our surroundings. For example, it can be hard to see yourself worthy of scoring a million-dollar account when you have pennies in the bank. We've all heard of people buying watches, suits and cars, all to impress upon the people they interact with their worthiness to be included in a deal. The truth is, some may need those material trappings because their confidence is linked to the items listed.

UNDERSTANDING that you are worthy of your desires regardless of your current financial state is key, because it will draw your desires to you, and it's much cheaper. You shouldn't have to buy a car to find the confidence you need to go after your destiny. Money, clothes, jewelry, cars, and even trophy wives are best if used in their proper place: as rewards for hard work. If you use this formula backwards, your success will be tied to the "things" you possess, and is always subject to being taken away. You must strengthen your mind so that regardless of the automobile in your driveway or the watch on your wrist, you know YOU have the ability to create the life you desire.

3

Day 3

Affirmation:

I POSSES WITHIN ME EVERYTHING NEEDED TO MANIFEST THE DESTINY THAT I CHOOSE.

EVERYTHING YOU NEED IS ALREADY within you. Don't wait for others to light your fire. You have your own matches.
— Unknown

HAVE you ever had an idea and instead of acting on it you shared it with others close to you? Once they agreed or suggested the same idea, you felt better about moving forward. It took their external validation to make you appreciate your instinctive brilliance. This must stop if you wish to reach your true potential.

A MENTALLY WEAK person values the opinions of others over their internal voice, whereas a mentally strong person puts their internal voice first. You must accept that everything you needed to achieve your ultimate success was within you when your mother birthed you. Did you have the training, knowledge and experience? Of course not, but you possessed the ability to get everything needed to reach your full potential on your first birthday.

THE ONLY THING that can propel you through the obstacles and hard work needed to accomplish your goals is having a strong mental capacity. Doctors and lawyers will tell you there is no magic formula they took that led to them persevering through the long study hours and complicated exams. They persevered through endless classwork while others were leading less complicated lives, to say the least. The only thing that propels some through monotony and hard work is mental fortitude.

4

Day 4

Affirmation:

I AM BLESSED AND CONSTANTLY FIND FAVOR WITH OTHERS.

SEDUCTION IS A GAME OF PSYCHOLOGY, not beauty, and it is within the grasp of any person to become a master at the game.

— Robert Greene, The Art of Seduction

THE ENTERTAINMENT INDUSTRY is built on our need for acceptance from others. If you've ever heard the saying that "Fame is a drug," it means that once a person has tasted the feeling of mass approval, it's hard for them to ever go back.

. . .

MOST OF US aren't celebrities, but we still feed off of the approval of others. If our co-workers show us appreciation we are more likely to share ideas at work. If a salesperson flirts with us we are more likely to make a purchase. There are two huge issues with this way of thinking.

THE FIRST IS that the way we interpret approval from others is often flawed. Co-workers may treat us with kindness because they don't see us as a threat. A salesperson may be flirtatious because they are in a good mood or just got a huge bonus. We can't be certain that a person is treating us with kindness because they like us. It could be for reasons that have nothing to do with us at all.

THE SECOND REASON we cannot rely on this thinking is that psychology shows us there are things anyone can do to appear more favorable with others. I'm not suggesting everyone enlist the processes outlined in 'The Art of Seduction' but conditioning your mind to expect the favor of others is the first step in creating that reality.

5

Day 5

Affirmation:

I EMBRACE MY PASSION REALIZING IT IS LEADING ME TOWARDS A HIGHER VERSION OF MYSELF.

FOLLOW YOUR PASSION, *it will lead you to your purpose.*

— *Oprah Winfrey*

IT'S hard to fight your passion. If you are currently fighting yours, I guarantee you are highly dysfunctional in more ways than one. The energy it takes for a person to fight their passion carries them into depression and unfailing self-doubt. The reason behind this is that your passion comes to you easily. When you go against it, you are working twice as hard to get to go half as far.

PASSION IS DEFINED as a strong feeling of enthusiasm or excitement for something or about something. That enthusiasm and excitement acts as a virtual gas pedal accelerating you faster toward your destiny. While it may take hard work to perfect it, the work won't feel as strenuous as if you are pursuing something that doesn't internally drive you.

AS WE CONTINUE to build your mental confidence you will realize that what comes naturally is your authentic truth. When you are truly in line with your personal truth, the vision for your destiny may change from what you originally envisioned. If that happens, trust the process, remember you are becoming a different version of yourself. There are many things that will change and I encourage you to embrace it. Change is a part of progress. If you feel yourself changing, it's a good sign you are moving in the right direction.

6

Day 6

Affirmation:

MY PAST CIRCUMSTANCES AND MY PRESENT SITUATION DON'T DICTATE THE POTENTIAL OF MY FUTURE.

BEFORE YOU CAN LIVE *a part of you has to die. You have to let go of what could have been. How you should've acted and what you wish you would have said differently. You have to accept that you can't change the past experiences, opinions of others at that moment in time or outcomes from their choices or yours. When you finally recognize that truth, then you will understand the true meaning of forgiveness of yourself and others. From this point you will finally be free.*

— Shannon L. Alder

. . .

OVERCOMING your own circumstances and or history is one of the most mentally challenging feats many of us encounter. I find it interesting that failing early in life is one of the best things that happened to most successful people.

I HAVE a good friend who became a multimillionaire before age 40, and in many of our conversations I've asked him what the determining factor was in his pursuit of success. You may expect me to share that he came from a loving family and a stable background, complete with a strong support system and superior education. Instead my friend's story is the exact opposite: rather than growing up in a loving family unit, his father passed away when he was in elementary school, leaving him and his siblings with a single mom struggling to survive. Instead of encouraging him, his mom constantly reminded him that he was destined to be a failure. The majority of his environment growing up served as a continual reminder that he was supposed to lose in life. His mentality was strong enough to overcome those messages early on, so when he encountered personal mistakes, failures, and ridicule etc. later in life his skin was tough enough for those obstacles not to penetrate his psyche.

THE FASTER YOU can overcome your past and realize it

has nothing to do with your worth or ability the faster you will be on your way to a new life.

7

Day 7

Affirmation:

EVERY SITUATION IN MY LIFE IS WORKING ON MY PERSONAL BEHALF!

NOURISH what makes you feel confident, connected, content. Opportunity will rise to meet you.

— Oprah Winfrey

CONGRATULATIONS ON BEING FINISHED with your first week! You are on your way to welcoming a new normal in your life. This is the epiphany that will change the vibration of everything you encounter from this point on.

As you do your meditation every morning, I hope you

find yourself re\visiting your affirmations throughout the day as a way to deal with any inconsistencies you may encounter.

ONE OF MY favorite gospel songs goes "*All things are working for me, even things I cannot see.*" If I had a penny for every time I've heard people say that everything is against them. We believe because of our race, physical attributes, culture, gender or family that the world is against us. Believing that everything and everyone is against you is a victim's mindset that excuses you from taking accountability for your own shortcomings. From this day forward, instead of entertaining thoughts of who is against you, you speak your new truth that all things are working on your behalf.

YOU ARE NOT A VICTIM. You do not have a victim's mindset. Speak your truth and watch as your circumstances and those around you become aligned with this reality.

8

Day 8

Affirmation:

I STRIVE FOR GREATNESS AND ACHIEVE IT. I DO NOT FEAR THE JOURNEY BECAUSE I KNOW IT'S PREPARING ME FOR MY END GOAL.

"IF YOU WANT to be great at something, there's a choice you have to make. What I mean by that is, there are inherent sacrifices that come along with that. Family time, hanging out with friends, being a great friend, being a great son, nephew, whatever the case may be."

— Kobe Bryant

WELCOME TO DAY 8. Greatness is the only option! At the beginning of 2020, basketball great Kobe Bryant passed away in a freak helicopter accident with his teenage daughter. The entire nation mourned Bryant's passing— even those who didn't play or even relate to the game of basketball. Bryant's star was bigger than basketball because of his dedication to excellence in everything he did, which has been called the "Mamba mentality."

KOBE'S COMMITMENT to greatness influenced everyone who watched him play, and in death it has proven to be his biggest impact. His intolerance of anything other than excellence was one of the things that irritated his teammates on the court but made them revere him later. The same was said about Michael Jordan and most athletes that reach the level of greatness that Kobe Bryant did. It's impossible to reach that point of success without overcoming both your fear and your natural avoidance of hard work.

I spent time in the studio with Polow da Don, one of the music industry's most successful producers. Polow is one of those rare individuals that, like Kobe Bryant, is completely sold on the journey of chasing greatness. Most people with this philosophy have little patience or empathy for others that aren't sold-out in the way that they are. I watched Polow do 48-hour stints at the studio after he'd earned the title super producer because he was committed to the pursuit of greatness. Junior producers would arrive at the studio hours after he would and leave hours before, and he would suggest to everyone in his smug demeanor, "they don't want to be great." His arrogance was often a point of contention with colleagues but his dogged determination to be in consistent pursuit of greatness is the fiber that creates legends.

THIS CONCEPT ISN'T RESERVED for athletes or musicians or any specific field or genre. We all have the opportunity to commit to the pursuit of greatness, and once you make the commitment, there are no excuses and no room for anything less.

9

Day 9

Affirmation:

EVERYONE IN MY LIFE IS AN ALIGNMENT WITH MY RENEWED PURPOSE AND GOALS.

THE UNIVERSE DOES this thing where it aligns you with people, things and situations that match the energy you put out. The more you improve yourself and raise your vibration, the more you will see things that are beneficial to your well-being.

— *Unknown*

ONE OF THE biggest deterrents to our achieving mental immunity is the noise caused by other people. Too often we allow others' motives or intentions to preoccupy our thoughts. We spend so much time focusing on who is coming in our lives or going out of our lives that it distracts us from being productive. There is no way you can know the motives of another person regardless of how long you've known them or even if they came into your life via someone else you trust. Instead of worrying about others' motives or agendas, it's best to focus on moving toward your goal and knowing the universe will bring those needed to assist you in reaching this goal, and in the same token will remove those who aren't in your company for the right reasons.

PAYING TOO much attention to others actions is a surefire way to waste time and energy. One of the benefits of developing a strong mental immunity is that distractions from others will be inconsequential to you. When we know that our focus and determination to move forward are the key ingredients to our success, we can release our fascination with others, whether their intentions are helpful or harmful. When we fully grasp the idea that our final destination is approved, the fear of someone else infiltrating that is removed and we can welcome those that come into our space with the understanding that if they are not in alignment with our higher destiny they will be removed.

10

Day 10

Affirmation:

I AM MORE POWERFUL THAN ANY OBSTACLE THAT ENTERS MY PATH.

I AM STRONG BEYOND BELIEF. I am powerful beyond measure.

— Abby Ruby

IT'S Day 10 and this is one of my favorite affirmations. I hope it will be one of your favorites as well. Today's affirmation is the foundation upon which this entire exercise is based. Once you start to view yourself as more powerful than any obstacle, then you will start to see life from a different perspective.

EARLY IN MY career I was complaining to my uncle about needing to make payroll. I had a small staff of three account executives and my payroll for that week was around fifty-five hundred dollars. I had clients that were consistently late with payments and it was stressing my overall business. I expected my uncle to empathize with me and realize how overwhelmed I was as an entrepreneur. Instead of sympathizing with me, my uncle laughed at the amount of money that was causing me stress. An entrepreneur himself, he shared that his payroll for the week was forty thousand dollars and he too was struggling, but he wasn't in a defeated state like I was. "The question is, do you think you are larger than that fifty-five hundred dollars or do you think that amount is bigger than you?" I didn't know how to respond. "There are two types of people in this world," he explained. "Successful people see themselves as bigger than their problems. Unsuccessful people see their problems as bigger than themselves. Which one are you?"

THIS WAS a pivotal conversation in my life. I decided right then and there that I was always going to see myself as bigger than any obstacle I faced. Of course, I would be able to make payroll because my uncle was right, fifty-five hundred dollars was more than manageable. He too was able to make his payroll but as we both learned, the more success that comes your way, the bigger the obstacles become.

UNLESS YOU ENVISION yourself as larger than your immediate problems, you will never be ready to elevate to the next level. Be it financial issues, emotional issues or even your own mistakes, you must see yourself as large and capable of handling anything life throws your way. Until you master this, you will never be ready for the next level the universe is waiting for you to achieve.

11

Day 11

Affirmation:

I SPEAK WITH WISDOM AND AUTHORITY, AND OTHERS RESPECT ME.

RESPECT yourself and others will respect you.
— Confucius

WORKING with horses is my favorite hobby. I learned early on that horses have a pretty sophisticated way of deciding who gets to claim leader. With my first horse, a mare named Paris, I tried over and over to get her to do what I wanted when I was on her back or on the ground. She was an eight-year-old Arabian mix and as I soon learned she was pretty head smart. One day while I was trying to get her to go into one of the smaller pastures, she kept turning me around so that we were headed back to the barn. I kicked and prodded and begged her to no avail. One of the stable hands saw me struggling with her and he laughed. Angrily, I asked him why I couldn't get the horse to go where I wanted. "Did you tell her to do it?" He asked. "Of course," I replied. "She doesn't believe you are the leader," he explained. It turned out, my actions and words weren't relaying to my horse that I was confident in my direction. Since she didn't feel I was confident in my leadership skills, she had no intention of following my instructions (As I mentioned earlier, she was a really smart horse).

CONFIDENCE IS something that you can't replicate: it comes from within. If you don't see yourself as trustworthy or respectable, you can be sure others won't see you that way either. Often it's not that we don't see ourselves that way, it's just that others are picking up on our self-doubt. I really wanted that horse to go into the small pasture, I just wasn't sure she would listen to me.

IF YOU HAVE TAKEN this attitude into your job, or any other area of your life, you have more than likely dealt with similar circumstances.

The answer to my problem wasn't to change my horse.

She was following her instinct. If she was to follow someone that wasn't a good leader, it could eventually result in her hurting herself or the person she was carrying. By the same logic, it doesn't make sense for others to respect a person who doesn't unequivocally respect themselves. It's an undeserved luxury. Earn your respect by first respecting yourself. It's a universal law that others will have no choice but to do the same.

12

DAY 12

Affirmation:

I AM AN ASSET TO EVERYONE IN MY PERSONAL AND BUSINESS NETWORK.

I GO crazy trying to energize people, cause that's what I am. I am a battery. If you're down, you can plug into me and get charged up.

— *Eli Manning*

IF YOU'VE EVER HAD the pleasure of being around a truly positive person, you can admit their energy at some point threatened to spill over into your energy. You may not have felt up to it at the time, and you may have even rejected it, but positivity is something that's impossible to keep to one's self.

ALTHOUGH CHILDREN rarely play outside on playgrounds anymore, most of us remember having physical education class at school and the task of picking a team. The first chosen are usually the most athletic, the next are the kids that are just fun to be around. The last chosen are the clumsy, shy and socially awkward kids. Most of the children in the latter bunch have no self-confidence and wouldn't pick themselves to be on a team if they had the chance. I'm not sure where you were in that equation, but if it wasn't in the preferred group, you have an excuse in that you were a child. You no longer are a child and it's time to step up and be that strong and effective captain for your team.

YOU MAKING the commitment to stabilize your mental immunity inevitably benefits those around you. By bolstering your ability to consistently be present and productive, you are giving an invaluable gift to those around you. Family, friends and even co-workers will reap immeasurable benefits as you will have re-directed the energy coming towards you. Those surrounding you or affiliated with you cannot help but reap the benefits from this.

13

Day 13

Affirmation:

MY INTERNAL PEACE IS UNSHAKABLE AND UNAFFECTED BY WHAT IS HAPPENING AROUND ME.

PEACE COMES FROM WITHIN. Don't seek it without.

— Buddha

SINCE STARTING this process you have had to find a quiet place to recite your affirmations every day. One of the reasons this is a part of the process is because it allows you to connect with your inner peace. I'm not sure our instincts have us looking to external sources when we are upset, sad or anxious.

WE TREAT our anxiety and sadness with alcohol, drugs, shopping, sex and so many other vices that distract us from our internal turmoil. If you've ever attempted to find peace in a bottle of alcohol, a joint or even another person, then you know real peace was not there. Yes, you probably experienced a temporary numbing sensation that gave your mind a break and allowed you to forget for a short period of time. But inevitably when the high wore off, you sobered up, the other person left and/or your credit card statement showed up, and you realized without the distraction you are right back where you started with the same internal turmoil (and probably less money in your pockets and a potential addiction brewing).

THE REASON that those vices won't work is because what you are seeking is already within you. Instead of running to the liquor store or to the mall or someone's bed, you need to dig deep within yourself to uncover that calm beneath the surface.

AUTHOR and inspirational speaker Iyanla Vanzant often

speaks about the importance of "breathing". She says, "Breathing deeply and releasing fear will help you get to where you want to be." As simple as those instructions are, they are the key to quieting your inner turmoil and reconnecting with your inner peace.

14

Day 14

Affirmation:

MY PURSUIT OF HAPPINESS IS PERFECTLY DESIGNED TO BLESS THOSE AROUND ME, NEAR AND FAR.

THE GREATNESS of a man is not how much wealth he acquires, but in his integrity and his ability to affect those around him positively.
— Bob Marley

THIS PROCESS WAS DESIGNED to unapologetically benefit YOU. I have found over the years that when people do things motivated by the need to help or serve others, their own progress often gets overlooked. People who put their needs first are often labeled as selfish or even narcissistic. The ironic thing that very few point out is that selfish or narcissistic people are usually extremely successful, and while they may need to work on empathy or compassion, I'd be willing to bet that many of them could state the affirmations in this book without blinking an eye.

IF YOU ARE OPERATING in the full capacity of your passion and following your purpose, those actions may at first feel selfish or self-serving— but life has a funny way of allowing everything at its best to bless others. A bright sun produces vitamin D which allows flowers to blossom, grass to grow and even nourishes you and I. You take sports heroes like Kobe Bryant or Michael Jordan, two people who consistently operated on their highest frequencies possible, and I don't have to convince you how many people their lives have blessed. Besides ticket holders and jobs created by their excellence on the court, there's the sheer fascination in a former high school basketball player watching these superhumans accomplish feats that they could only dream of doing. Their pursuit of happiness blessed those they were directly responsible for and hundreds of thousands of others who loved just watching them play.

Artists like Bob Marley, Celine Dion, Taylor Swift and Michael Jackson pursued their own happiness with their music and that pursuit continues to bless others.

. . .

YOUR JOURNEY to happiness has to be focused on conquering your mental stability and focus and, like the examples mentioned above, that end result will both directly and indirectly bless those around you.

15

Day 15

Affirmation:

THAT WHICH MAKES ME DIFFERENT MAKES ME VALUABLE.

I FIND that the very things that I get criticized for, which is usually being different and just doing my own thing and just being original, is the very thing that's making me successful.

— Shania Twain

FROM THE BEGINNING OF TIME, differences have separated human beings. Racial differences, physical differences, and religious differences have all resulted in separation at best, war at worst. Differences prohibit us from hiding amongst the crowd and alert us that we are being seen. Being seen prohibits us from hiding what we see as our flaws, but nine times out of ten our flaws or differences are what also make us special.

THE ENERGY SPENT HIDING your flaws works in direct opposition to exposing what will separate you from the crowd and eventually signify your value. It's ironic that we work so hard to fit in, even though the ones that set the trends do so by standing out. Whether it's Julia Roberts' toothy grin, Lady Gaga's socially awkward brilliance or Kevin Hart's diminutive stature, their differences worked to make them superstars amongst stars.

IF YOU THINK BACK to your high school days and consider the people that stood out, they were all people with differences that were celebrated. Sure, there were the best athletes, those that displayed above average talent, but then there were also the students that were just different. I would be willing to bet you remember the tallest girl, the shortest guy. People that are different are the ones that stand out in our memory, which means they are the ones who make an impression. The sooner you figure out how to embrace that which makes you different, the sooner you will find your superpower and understand how to use it to your advantage.

. . .

I DECIDED to hyphenate my name after my first marriage . After moving back to my hometown I started applying for jobs, and I remember thinking the hyphenated name was a pain because it was longer than most and didn't fit neatly in the resume templates I was using. I was applying for public relations positions, a very appearance-driven field, so I was careful to make sure my resumes were visually appealing. For my first crop of resumes I applied to ten different positions. I sent cover letters and resumes to all ten HR managers. Out of ten resumes I received eight callbacks. Surprisingly one of the first things every recruiter I spoke with mentioned was the fact that my name stood out and made me seem interesting.

INSTEAD OF SHYING AWAY from the things that make you different, leaning into them and highlighting them is the first step in connecting with your superpowers.

Day 16

Affirmation:

I AM COMMITTED TO FINDING THE POSITIVE IN EVERY SITUATION AND ENCOUNTER.

WE CAN COMPLAIN because rose bushes have thorns or rejoice because thorns have roses.

— *Alphonse Karr*

YOU ARE UNSTOPPABLE! I know this is true because you are more than halfway through this exercise and you haven't given up. I know that you are unstoppable but that isn't what is most important. What's most important is that by now you have figured that out yourself.

. . .

KNOWING who you are is the BIGGEST step in changing your life, and the follow-up to that is having the ability to look at every situation from a positive perspective. This can be challenging for even the strongest of mentalities, but it can be done.

NOT FOR ONE minute am I suggesting that tragedies like death, divorce, financial loss and illnesses, just to name a few, aren't worthy of grieving and don't cause tremendous, overwhelming heartache. What I am suggesting is that life unfortunately doesn't give us a grace period for handling those world-altering events. Because life goes on, we have to train our brains to operate in a way that will acknowledge pain and disappointment but NOT break down. To ask someone to acknowledge death and then to look at it from a positive perspective is a tall order, but I'm telling you that it's an important part of training yourself to remain in a positive state.

DEATH and other tragedies are a part of life which means we know we'll have to deal with them time and time again. We must put a failsafe in place in order to deal with these tragedies without losing our sense of self.

. . .

IN THE SPRING of 2020 a global pandemic has dominated the entire world. Jobs were lost, lives were lost and yet I sit here after losing one of my last clients writing this book for you. Why, you might ask? Because this pandemic has taught us that life has the ability to strip every external thing from you without warning. During these times, if you don't have a strong mental immune system you will break. Your mental fortitude can be built to withstand pain even when your heart cannot.

AS LONG AS you have breath in your body, you have the opportunity to build once more, to chase a dream, to experience love, to create the life that you desire. You are more than halfway there!

17

Day 17

Affirmation:

I CELEBRATE MY PERSONAL HISTORY, AS IT CREATED THE DNA I NEEDED TO BECOME A SUCCESS.

EVEN IN DEFEAT *there is a valuable lesson learned, so it evens up for me.*

—Jay Z

THERE ARE numerous variables that connect us in the human struggle. We all have a beginning and we will all have an end. Most of us have experiences in our past that we aren't proud of and that we may even try to forget.

Childhood trauma, family secrets, and personal failures color our pasts and act as stumbling blocks that often prevent us from moving forward. But the truth is, every single experience you've come through has prepared you for your success.

RAPPER-TURNED-ENTERTAINMENT billionaire Jay Z was born into humble beginnings. What makes Jay Z different is he is one of those rare people born with a mental immunity that couldn't be compromised. His innate ability to repel the negativity he experienced in school and the environment he was immersed in enabled him to propel himself out of his native environment and gave him the protection he needed to navigate the often treacherous entertainment industry. He gave the above-mentioned quote when speaking on his past failures and disappointments. He was able to focus on the lessons learned during these failures and use the knowledge gained to fund new successes.

MANY PEOPLE IDOLIZE JAY Z, Warren Buffet, Oprah, Bill Gates and other icons of extreme success. We place them on pedestals,all the while thinking there must be something about them that's different from ourselves. It's comforting to think that they had things easier than we do or someone gave them a handout that we haven't received.

While those thoughts ease our conscience, they are wrong and work to keep us stuck in mediocrity.

JAY Z GIVES the secret to his success throughout many of his interviews: it's his ability to interpret his failures as lessons and not as definitions of his identity or ability. This is a powerful mantra and will work for anyone who applies it.

Day 18

Affirmation:

I RISE TO EVERY CHALLENGE AND EMBRACE HARD WORK AS A GIFT THAT PUSHES ME CLOSER TO MY HIGHER SELF!

IF A MAN CHOOSES a certain way and seems to have no particular talent for this way, he can still become a master if he so chooses. By keeping at a particular form of study a man can attain perfection either in this life or the next.

— Miyamoto Musashi

THE ABILITY TO get up in the morning and start all over,

and then do the same thing again and again and again requires both discipline and a strong sense of self. To push oneself over and over without immediate return on ones' investment takes a personal resolve that many don't have. Still, it's that same resolve that guarantees you will one day reach your goals.

YOU MAY BE familiar with the theory Malcom Gladwell presents in his book, *Outliers* which states that 10,000 hours of practice at any craft can turn anyone into an expert. The number of hours on your journey towards your final destination may be more or less than that, but what is not debatable is the equation that hard work equals progress. Without sacrifice and sweat you will never reach your goals. Knowing this, you should welcome hard work, as it's leading you closer to where you want to be.

WHEN WE ARE WORKING on our physical appearance, we know the pain experienced from sore muscles and stiff joints will eventually yield the results we are seeking. Personal trainers and coaches often congratulate you if you are in pain because the pain is proof that you put in the kind of work that will show up later. When you feel that physical burn, you know that you did a great job with your workout. The same is true for the hard work we put in moving towards our goals and dreams. We should look forward to feeling that fatigue as proof that we are that much closer to our destiny of choice.

19

Day 19

Affirmation:

EVERY DAY THE UNIVERSE GIVES ME AN OPPORTUNITY TO BECOME BETTER. EACH DAY BEGINS AND ENDS AS IT SHOULD.

EMBRACE the high truth that everything comes to pass exactly as it should. Find peace and wisdom by accepting what is.

— Dan Millman

ONCE YOU KNOW that you've put in the hard work discussed in the previous affirmation, your next step is to trust that the universe has met you where you are and will do the rest. Wake up each day knowing that you have an opportunity to give your all. At the end of each day accept that the day went exactly as it played out. Philosopher Nayyirah Waheed states this perfectly with the quote, "*Be easy. Take your time. You are coming home to yourself.*

THIS EXERCISE IS all about learning to trust yourself while trusting the universe. Another way to define this is living by faith. The Bible defines faith in Hebrews 11:1 as "Faith is the substance of things hoped for, the evidence of things not seen."

FAITH IS KNOWING that although you may not see change today, you know that the hard work you put in combined with the dedication to remain positive regardless of the situation or circumstance will ignite the universe to return that energy sevenfold.

20

Day 20

Affirmation:

I POSSESS THE TIME AND THE ABILITY TO ACCOMPLISH MY GOALS.

WE ALL HAVE ABILITY. The difference is how we use it.

— Stevie Wonder

QUESTIONING our ability is something we all have done at one point or another. Most of the time it's not so much that we are questioning ourselves, but more that we have attached an image to our idea of success and then compared ourselves to that image. If I want to be a pop star and I see that Beyonce is a pop star, it's easy for me to find things about Beyonce that don't line up with myself and doubt my own ability.

THIS THINKING IS FLAWED on many levels, though it's a basic human instinct to compare ourselves to others. If legendary artist and musician Stevie Wonder had compared himself to his contemporaries, he would never have become an icon. Not only was Wonder not the same race as most of his fellow musicians, but he was also blind.

ALL AROUND US we see examples of people overcoming mind-blowing obstacles to accomplish their goals, from Olympiads with handicaps to government officials with prior learning disabilities. It's clear that we ALL, regardless of where we begin, have the ability to achieve our goals. Your journey may take more time than someone else's, but that's not what you should be focused on. You should be focused on your journey and the hard knowledge that you have the ability to get there. You also need to know that there is no set time clock on your achievement. With each milestone you accomplish, know you are arriving right on time. Your schedule for success belongs to you alone.

21

Day 21

Affirmation:

I AM IN PERFECT HARMONY WITH THE UNIVERSE AND THE UNIVERSE IS IN PERFECT HARMONY WITH ME.

TRUTH IS INNER HARMONY.

— *Walther Rathenau*

IT TAKES twenty-one days to create a habit. You have created a habit of repeating affirmations specifically curated to establish a mental immunity that will assist you with dealing with life's continuous ups and downs. Today's affirmation is important because it assures us again that we are indeed exactly where we are supposed to be on this day at this time.

IT TAKES us surrendering our egos to realize that everything in our lives is as it should be. We are moving at the pace that has already been predestined for our lives. Everything we encounter from people we meet, even to YOU getting a copy of this book is already mapped out for you. All you have to do is surrender to that inner voice and accept your reality as the perfect place for you today.

ANXIETY IS the culprit that often keeps us from accepting we are in perfect harmony with the universe and that it is working on our behalf. It is often caused by an assumption that we should be somewhere else or doing something else. We spend hours comparing ourselves with others and our egos makes us feel insignificant or unsatisfied with our current reality. If we are living in our truth, we learn to acknowledge that everything that comes into our path works to push us towards our destiny.

LIVING in your truth requires you to be in complete authenticity at all times. Once you reject your ego and embrace your truth, you will see that the universe is indeed working on your behalf: all you have to do is stay the course.

22

Day 22

Affirmation:

UNCONDITIONAL LOVE STARTS WITHIN ME AND FLOWS FREELY FROM ME AND BACK TO ME.

SHINE your soul with the same egoless humility as the rainbow and no matter where you go in this world, or the next, love will find you, attend you and bless you.

— *Aberjhani*

LOVE AND SUPPORT are not luxuries: they are both needed for survival. When we are young, we look to our parents for love and support. As teenagers we tend to look towards our friends and peers, and as we enter adulthood we often look for them in a significant other. There is, however, no guarantee that we'll receive love and support from any of the sources from which we seek it. The lack of love and support from a parent or parents is one of the biggest contributors to self-doubt. If for whatever reason our parents are unable to provide us with the love and support we need as a child we interpret that we are somehow undeserving. When teenagers don't feel accepted or supported by peers, their self-esteem becomes compromised and, when left untreated, those wounds become a handicap in adulthood. Later as adults, we often feel mistreated or abandoned when we don't receive love and support from our significant others. Sometimes their intention isn't to love or support us, while other times they want to but don't have the emotional fuel themselves to fill our tanks. Humans are flawed by nature, which is why it's dangerous to rely on another human being for anything survival based.

I DON'T MEAN to suggest that we don't need others, because that's certainly not true, but once you learn to provide love and support for yourself, you will never again be at the mercy of another human being. If you are able to provide unconditional love and support for yourself you will not only have a huge advantage in life, but you will draw that same love and support like a magnet from others. The best way to give others permission to love and support you is if they see you celebrating yourself unconditionally. Once you master this, you will feel love within your very existence and anything someone else offers can be an appreciated luxury.

23

Day 23

Affirmation:

PATIENCE IS A VIRTUE THAT RESIDES WITHIN ME.

PATIENCE IS the calm acceptance that things can happen in a different order than the one you have in your mind.

— David G. Allen

THE EGO IS the opposite of patience, which is why we must rid ourselves of it in order to establish mental stability. You are probably silently rejecting the idea of having an ego but believe it or not, we all have one. When we place time restraints on our goals, it's our ego suggesting that we should be at a certain place at a certain time. Patience assures us that hard work will yield a harvest in due time. Our ego suggests if we don't arrive by our self-imposed deadline then we are unworthy of and perhaps incompetent at achieving our goals.

MY GRANNY DIDN'T SPEAK VERY OFTEN but when she did it was often to point out the mistakes of either my Mother,myself, or one of her other children. I recall speaking to her as a proud college graduate and telling her my ten-year plan. I spoke with false confidence, speckled with the fear that if I didn't achieve certain goals by age thirty, I wouldn't consider myself a success. My Granny would laugh at my plans and tell me that it was nice to dream but life didn't always work the way we wanted it to. I'll be honest, her responses used to irritate me as I was in my early twenties and convinced that I could force my way to success. It took me many years, after my grandmother had long succumbed to Alzheimer's, to realize that she did believe in me. Her words were directed at my impatience and not my ability to achieve my goals.

I WAS right about the ability to force my way to success, but I was very wrong about putting absolute deadlines on both the short- and long-term goals. My ego demanded that I accomplish certain goals in order to feel a sense of self-satisfaction. That same ego would turn on me if life had other plans and make me feel depressed or anxious at not being able to meet the self-imposed deadline.

WHEN PATIENCE IS OUR TEMPO, we are content to continue putting in hard work knowing that one of the laws of the universe is sowing and reaping. This universal truth allows us to live with patience as our guide, knowing beyond a shadow of a doubt that we will reach our destination at the perfect time.

24

Day 24

Affirmation:

I CAN ACKNOWLEDGE PAST AND FUTURE MISTAKES WITHOUT PENALIZING MYSELF FOR THEM. MY EXPERIENCE PUSHES ME FORWARD.

FAILURE DOESN'T DEFINE YOU. It's what you do after you fail that determines whether you are a leader or a waste of perfectly good air.

— *Sabaa Tahir, A Torch Against the Night*

WE'VE ALREADY CONQUERED the concept of mistakes being opportunities to learn and move forward. But we want to make sure that we don't penalize ourselves for those mistakes, which will enable others to use our mistakes against us. It's also important to understand that with hard work and progress there will be mistakes.

YOUR MISTAKES ARE unique opportunities to elevate yourself. I love this quote by Sabaa Tahir because it addresses the fact that it's imperative that leaders make mistakes in order to grow and develop their skill set. The key to turning your mistakes into valuable experience lies in your ability to rebound correctly. Before self-doubt creeps in you need to immediately stop and redirect your thought process. Leadership requires experiential lessons that prepare you for its responsibilities.

WE CELEBRATE when the stock trader gets a windfall, but no one talks about the many times he lost money and learned how to navigate the market. We celebrate when the basketball star hits the three-pointers, but we forget all of the air balls shot in order to perfect his game. Your misses give you the knowledge and strategy needed to become a winner.

25

Day 25

Affirmation:

MY SOUL RADIATES FROM WITHIN ALLOWING OTHERS TO SEE MY BEAUTY.

BEAUTY IS how you feel inside, and it reflects in your eyes. It's not something physical.

— Sophia Loren

MY COLLEGE THESIS was based on the science behind beauty and how science provides us with a formula also known as a standard of beauty. At twenty-one years old I was able to scientifically prove that symmetrical features and certain physical characteristics defined the parameters of beauty. My thesis suggested that those who were born with characteristics that lined up with the scientific standard of beauty received more job offers, raises, marriage proposals, etc. I was able to prove that beauty offered a huge advantage on all fronts: in work, life and love. My conclusion earned me a ninety one percent on the paper and was supported by magazines and the entire entertainment industry.

IRONICALLY, I learned through time and experience that the twenty-one-year-old college student version of myself was wrong. Not only was she wrong, but surprisingly all the books, papers and articles I researched were wrong right along with me. Life has a way of putting you in the lane to learn what you need to correct.

MY FASCINATION with beauty led me to becoming an entertainment publicist working among the beautiful people. As a shy young woman from Oklahoma, I often felt out of place on press junkets for television and music projects in New York, LA, Atlanta and Miami. I was constantly around women the world considered "most beautiful" and men that were considered "most desirable". I was frequently surprised to learn that these envied people were not as confident as one would imagine. Not only did many lack self-confidence, but some weren't kind and didn't treat others with respect.

The ones obsessed with themselves who weren't kind to others or who had nasty dispositions weren't treated the same as the ones with kind spirits and self-confidence. I witnessed firsthand how others responded to beautiful outsides with ugly insides and it wasn't what I expected.

WHAT I ALSO LEARNED IS THAT even in the superficial entertainment industry, people were attracted long-term to those with confidence and kindness. Unlike high cheekbones and broad shoulders, confidence and integrity acted as magnets, drawing others closer and offering unique perks.

WHILE I'M NOT SUGGESTING that scientific beauty doesn't play a part in attraction, it is a short-term appeal. True beauty comes from an internal attraction to characteristics that touch the soul.

26

Day 26

Affirmation:

I WILL NOT DIM MY LIGHT FOR ANY PERSON, PLACE, OR THING.

SOME PEOPLE NEED to hold certain beliefs about you so they'll be more comfortable. Don't let their beliefs dim your light., You're not here for their comfort.

—Jenna Korf

THE TYPE of self-confidence you are building will give you a certain audacity that may shock YOU. Having a strong sense of self gives you a different type of presence. It shows up in the way you enter a room, the way you address others and even the way they respond to you. If you are noticing that others are responding to you differently, take that as confirmation that you are transitioning into a higher version of YOU— the version that is designed to guide you to your true destiny.

OTHERS' reactions are what cause us to second-guess ourselves. When your confidence exposes someone else's insecurity, it can feel uncomfortable at first. Most of us don't enjoy the feeling of making others uncomfortable, so we find ways around it. Think back to the tallest person in your elementary school. Mostly likely you'll have memories of them attempting to hunch their shoulders to appear shorter because they didn't want to stand out, which would remind others that they are shorter. Unfortunately, instead of blending in with the shorter students, the tall student just looked like they had bad posture. The same is true for YOU when you attempt to dim your light in order to make others feel more comfortable.

YOUR DENIAL of your own light doesn't keep others from seeing it. Instead they see you as someone who isn't self-aware and can either be taken advantage of or underestimated. When you dim your light, not only are you doing yourself a huge disservice but it also sends a message that you are inauthentic because you are rejecting your truth.

That dishonesty works against you in many ways, both in pursuit of your goals and in your relationships with others.

AS WE MOVE towards connecting with our higher selves, it's important to reject the idea of ever operating as anything less than your authentic self.

27

Day 27

Affirmation:

NOTHING HAS THE POWER TO STOP ME FROM REACHING MY INTENDED POTENTIAL OR GOALS.

I'VE BEEN through hell and back, I have to be honest, and still I'm able to do what I do and nothing can stop me. No one can stop me, no matter what. I stop when I'm ready to stop. I will continue to move forward no matter what.

— *Michael Jackson*

ONE OF THE most important affirmations in this exercise is the declaration that NOTHING has the power to stop you from reaching your intended potential. It's such a powerful statement that it can be overwhelming to take in it's true meaning. Life is full of twists and turns and many of them can threaten to shake us to our very core. Death, natural disasters, physical ailments and extreme financial loss can be some of the hardest experiences to endure and, afterwards, to remain focused on moving forward.

THE TRUTH IS, these tragedies are exactly what mental immunity is preparing you for. Being able to stay focused and positive while you are performing at your best and your family is happy and healthy isn't a test of your mental immunity. Staying committed to the pursuit of greatness while you are on a winning streak doesn't exhibit strength. The true testament of strength is when you lose your foundation and you remain committed to moving forward without the luxury of financial security. The true testament of strength is when you lose one of the people closest to you, whether through death, divorce or another tragedy, and you are able to pick yourself up and continue moving forward. The silent knowledge that whether you have money or not, whether you have support or not, whether you have the love of your life or not, whether you have your own health or not, you will continue to move forward and will reach your intended potential is the true test of mental immunity.

. . .

LIKE A COMPUTER, our brains are able to be programmed. This is why in order to be successful we must make our brain stronger than our emotions, stronger than our feelings and stronger than our learned behavior. This process of reprogramming your brain rests on the concept that once you make up your mind to do something, there should be NOTHING that can stop you or redirect you from that path.

28

Day 28

Affirmation:

I EMBRACE CONSTRUCTIVE CRITICISM AS IT MOVES ME CLOSER TOWARDS MY HIGHER SELF.

THE FINAL PROOF *of greatness lies in being able to endure criticism without resentment.*

— *Elbert Hubbard*

THE ABILITY TO take criticism is one of the truest signs of maturity, and also suggests one has a solid sense of self. Once you possess this type of authentic confidence, constructive criticism is seen as either something with the potential to make you better) or something to be discarded without emotional investment.

THERE IS A SAYING that suggests artists are sensitive about their work. Personally, I've seen this to be true, but I would also have to acknowledge that most artists I've been around have not been confident in their work. Their passion drives them, but many seek approval from others to solidify confidence in their work. In order to elevate to our higher self, we must work on our self-confidence so that we are able to allow constructive criticism to make us better.

IF WE ARE NOT MATURE, we focus on the source of the criticism and look for ways to discredit the information. This blocks us from elevation because it doesn't allow us to see ourselves objectively. When we encounter criticism, we should examine it from a non-emotional place, detaching it completely from its source. For example, I've heard people say that married people should never take advice from single people. While it sounds like a good idea, it's an asinine statement. If a single person has sound advice, then a married person would benefit themselves and their relationship by taking the advice. Instead many married people will consider the source and, depending on how they feel about the person offering the criticism or that person's personal situation, they'll decide if they want to accept or reject the criticism. This process is completely backwards and prohibits growth.

WHEN WE RECEIVE CRITICISM, we should immediately disconnect the information from its source. The source is inconsequential and has no bearing on if the statement is true or false. If you remain connected to the source you miss the opportunity to grow from that input.

MOVING FORWARD, I challenge you to immediately and completely remove criticism from its source. Examine the statement from an objective point for truth and accuracy. Remove your ego in order to extract the lesson, if there is one being offered. If not, release the statement and the energy from which it came. If it does indeed offer beneficial information, be grateful for the opportunity to grow and mature. Level Up!

29

Day 29

Affirmation:

I AM THE MOST IMPORTANT FACTOR IN MY LIFE'S STORY. I AM MY FIRST PRIORITY!

NO ONE CARES about someone who's bent on self-sabotage. If you want to save the world from sinking, first pull yourself up and escape drowning.

— Unknown

PUTTING others before yourself can feel like an act of chivalry. From the outside looking in, it appears noble and garners much applause. Unfortunately, those who put others before themselves are usually creating a self-destructive pattern for themselves that ensures they will never reach their full potential. What's even more unfortunate is their inability to put themselves first means that those they are helping will likely be pushed to reach their highest potential either.

AS A PARENT I learned by default that the most impactful lesson you can give your child is the example you embody. Teaching your child to make his bed every morning is difficult to do if you don't make your bed every morning. Yes, you can yell and threaten punishment, but the day will come when that child will look you in the eyes and say, "Why do I have to make my bed when you don't make yours?"

THE SAME IS true for any lesson you attempt to give others. Encouraging others to strive for greatness is hypocritical if you aren't first striving for it yourself. There is a reason we're instructed on planes to first secure the oxygen mask on our own face before attempting to assist others. You will never be able to help others to the fullest extent if you are not operating as your highest self. It's not selfish to make yourself your first priority— in actuality it's the first step to personal success, which is needed in order to truly help others.

. . .

A POOR MAN may be noble, but he will never be able to help others as much as a man with means. You will never be able to truly help your family, friends, etc. until you secure your own position. Today, YOU break the pattern of feeling guilty or selfish for putting yourself first. YOU accept the idea that prioritizing your needs is the only way to guarantee personal success, and is therefore the only way to help others to the fullest extent of your abilities..

30

Day 30

Affirmation:

I REMAIN CALM UNDER PRESSURE AND STAY CONNECTED TO MY ULTIMATE PURPOSE.

IF YOU CAN REMAIN calm in the midst of great chaos, it is the surest guarantee that it will eventually subside.

—*Julie Andrews*

I LOVE the acronym that defines fear as false evidence appearing real, because it shows us that fear and anxiety are most often our emotions playing mind games with us. Yes, fear and anxiety are tangible feelings often stemming from palpable difficulties, but most often we extend more energy being anxious or afraid than we do actually dealing with the issue at hand. Remaining calm, continuing to breathe and staying connected to your purpose allows you to isolate the problem so that you can deal with it objectively and move forward.

WE EXPERIENCE FEAR AND/OR anxiety when we are not in control of an outcome. That feeling of helplessness can be crippling and even paralyzing. We've all felt it no matter gender, age, race or occupation. Strengthening your mental immunity means that you develop the ability to respond to fear without emotion. You become so convinced that the universe is moving on your behalf and your ultimate outcome is secure that anything along that journey is not to be feared, because ultimately it will be worked out in your favor. Your appointment with your higher self is your assurance that regardless of what comes your way, it will work out in your best interest.

FOR EXAMPLE: I may fear losing my job, but if I know that ultimately, regardless of what happens in this moment, nothing can stop me from reaching my appointment with destiny, I no longer feel helpless. I can rest assured knowing that things are being working out in my favor regardless of the short-term situation.

. . .

IN ORDER TO reach your greatest potential, you must not respond emotionally to triggers or even circumstances. It's important to remain calm and collected in order to make smart decisions and move through obstacles without adding additional setbacks. This only happens when we learn that fear is merely our interpretation of not having control over a situation.

31

Day 31

Affirmation:

I HAVE EMPATHY FOR OTHERS WITHOUT ABSORBING THEIR ISSUES BECAUSE MY DESTINY IS UNIQUELY MINE.

NO ONE CAN CREATE *negativity or stress within you. Only you can do that by virtue of how you process your world.*

— *Wayne Dyer*

HAVE you ever met someone who complained about their coworkers at consecutive jobs? Or do you have friends who constantly blame others for their mishaps, even though they've gone through numerous groups of friends? With these types of people, it is an afterthought to hold themselves responsible for their situation because they've convinced themselves that their issues are all the fault of someone else. This is a dangerous way of thinking, as it prevents you from taking one of the biggest steps towards personal success: accountability.

WHEN I AM MENTALLY STRONG, my friend's sadness cannot rub off on me. When I am in control of my thoughts, my coworkers complaining doesn't ruin my day. I am able to connect and communicate with others without absorbing their issues or emotions. If you constantly find yourself absorbing the internal issues of others, this is a sure sign that you aren't in sync with your true self. People with a strong sense of self are so convinced of who they are that no matter who they are surrounded by, they remain true to their own convictions and beliefs.

BEING EMPATHETIC TO OTHERS' struggles or pain does not equate to absorbing them. Once you absorb someone's pain or conflict, you are no longer a help to them but instead have become a handicap. A true sign of strength is being able to understand someone's pain and look for ways to assist them without becoming a victim to the pain ourselves. Strength lifts without succumbing: it's a branch that's able to bend to lend a listening ear, but not break under the pressure.

AS OUR MENTAL immunity becomes stronger, we are able to be a bigger asset to ourselves, and therefore a bigger asset to those around us.

Afterword

Congratulations! You have taken one of the biggest steps in elevating to your higher self. You probably feel as if you can take on the entire world without fear right now, and the truth is you can.

You have successfully re-programmed your internal thought processes, which is the single most important tool in creating the mental armor you need to navigate the ups and downs on your journey toward success. You have learned the secret that every successful person knows, and that is that your internal motivation is your greatest ally!

The last thing I want to leave you with is the understanding that when you put this book down, the process IS NOT

OVER! You will need to continue to work to keep your mind disciplined in this new way of thinking.

We know that computers often have to be re-booted and the same is true with our brains. You have started a great process that will need to be done over again as needed to keep you on track with all 31 of these affirmations.

My personal suggestion is to make them a part of your daily routine. Getting through the first thirty-one days was the first step but if you do not make every single one of these affirmations a way of life for the rest of your life, then you will be vulnerable to slipping back into a negative mode of dealing with emotions and mental weaknesses. Your mind is no different than your body, and if you do not continue to build and work your muscles then you will eventually lose the strength and resolve you've worked so hard to attain.

Whether or not you decide to continue will determine what type of future you create for yourself. In order to stay up, you must continue strengthening your mind and conditioning your thoughts. I've given you the tools to do it. It's game time, and the ball is in your court. I look forward to hearing your wins!

About the Author

Christal D. Jordan is an award-winning author and journalist. Jordan founded Enchanted Branding & Public Relations, one of the most in-demand entertainment public relations firms in the southeast.

In all of her pursuits, Jordan maintains a strong belief in women's empowerment and social development, manifesting in her first novel, Under the Cherry Moon and more recently In her role as a Relationship and Women's Issue editor for Rolling Out Magazine.

Further, she also hosts a YouTube series and a webisode series titled "Reality Check" for the magazine and does bi-weekly pop culture segments for Fox 5 Atlanta. Jordan is the mother of two children and is an avid equestrian in her free time. You can subscribe to her YouTube page by following her YouTube channel: EnchantedPRonline.

www.ingramcontent.com/pod-product-compliance
Lightning Source LLC
LaVergne TN
LVHW091120150826
845673LV00002B/911
* 9 7 8 0 5 7 8 6 8 8 0 8 4 *